A Guide to Internet Safety for Children, Teens & Young Adults

An Ideal Gift From Parents To Their Internet-savy Child

By

Rajesh Laskary

Author - Rajesh Laskary

Edited by - Anurag Kushwaha

Designer - Richa Bargotra

DISCLAIMER

Although the author and publisher have made every effort to ensure that the information in this book was correct at press time, the author and publisher do not assume and hereby disclaim any liability to any party for any loss, damage, or disruption caused by errors or omissions, whether such errors or omissions result from negligence, accident, or any other cause.

You should seek the services of a competent professional or expert in the field for anything specific. This book is presented solely for educational and informational purposes. The author and publisher are not offering it as any professional advice. The information in this book is meant to supplement your efforts to educate your children on various internet safety-related aspects.

PREFACE

In the last few years, we have started to read and listen to the news on someone getting duped with some online scam, tricked on social media, cyberbullied by a stranger, threatened online, and so on. The most threatening part of this is, the children and young adults have been most vulnerable to these online threats.

I have tried to put together a few essential tips that the children and young adults should know to be safe while browsing the internet, be safe while interacting with friends, families and also handling strangers online. Please understand that this is not a comprehensive list. You should always keep yourself updated by reading regularly about current events and incidents taking place in the cyber world, know and follow the best practices of cyber/internet security and also DOs & DON'Ts of Internet.

Knowing about such best practices will not only help us being safe online, but we will also be in a better position to safeguard our loved ones.

Contents

PART ONE

Chapter 1

What is the Internet?

Concisely and straightforwardly, internet refers to the "Network of Networks" connected having plenty of information stored, transmitted or processed on these networks that are interlinked on a full scale and are used by several people who are termed as 'users'.

You all might have read this definition or a similar one in your school textbooks and indeed know what internet means as it has been a part of your daily routine as well as those around you since you have been a kid.

While you can say that 'Google is what we call internet', it most certainly is not true even though most of what you do *on* the internet, revolves around search engines like Google and other applications. Internet on a bigger and broader scale is the intangible and unseen place where everything exists in the form of networks and is used by someone else being a part of that network.

At this age, you must be familiar and must have witnessed the enormous growth of the internet in the past years and must have been regularly seeing the news of another online business creating history or setting a new standard of innovation. All of what you do or see around you happening on the internet is just a small part of it that you in your day make use of. Further, in this book, we will be discussing more of the internet and why you need to be safe on it and what all can you do for that.

✐ **Points to Remember:**

- The Internet is a 'network of networks'.

- There has been an enormous growth of the internet from the 1990s till today, and many online businesses have flourished and witnessed benefits arising from it.

- Search engines like Google are just a part of the internet that help you find websites, data or anything in a database that is connected to world wide web (www) and the internet itself.

- You will be learning more about the internet and how you can be safe on it in the further chapters.

Chapter 2

What is Social Media?

Social Media is undoubtedly the most popular platform to connect, network and share data, media or talk online nowadays. Being a part of just another successful idea that was implemented on the internet, it is not an unknown fact that teenagers, adults and even children constitute a considerable part of social media.

Social interaction among people on the internet (it could be on websites or apps) in which they generate, share and exchange information, thoughts and content on internet communities via texts, images, videos. Facebook, LinkedIn, WhatsApp, Instagram are some famous examples of social media 'platforms'.

After unbelievably tremendous growth in Social Media, it is now an integral part of our internet world as almost all businesses, media houses, music industries and several artists have found a new way of exhibiting themselves to the world and gain more audience and make some good profit.

Even you might be very familiar with a lot of bloggers, vloggers, gaming artists, song artists and photographers who have achieved fame with social media and are no less popular than the film actors today! Most likely, you also might be already using many applications to talk to your friends and stay connected with them to share anything within seconds without much delay.

Those of you who are an active user of social media will most certainly find a lot of useful things to carry on with yourself and implement in this book that will lead to better, safer and more comfortable use of social media networks. To make sure you never fall in any trap and invite trouble, remember: internet might be easy to use and understand, but it is equally dangerous and unsafe because of some people who have the in-depth knowledge to manipulate the data and networks and make the young people their targets to make money or cheat them.

✍ **Points to Remember:**

- Such technical platforms that exist on the internet through which one can connect to people and share or create media files, information or news are social media networks.

- Some of the most famous examples are Instagram, Facebook, WhatsApp.

- Many businesses and individuals including bloggers or influencers have gained success, fame and built a massive audience through social media.

- However easy to use, the internet is equally dangerous and unsafe place due to some undesirable people who may take advantage of you and your data.

- You will also learn in the further chapters how you can safely and efficiently use social media without falling in some trap or causing trouble for yourself.

Chapter 3

How to Protect Your Personal Information Online?

So you learned about the internet and social media and know that you as an individual today of this generation, are an active part of both of them. Let's carry forward the topics and further make you familiar with what you do online and why you need to be secure on the internet and with whatever information you share and most certainly how easily can you be a safe user in the cyber world.

Your personal information is what belongs to you, that can be used to identify you (your name, email, company name, designation, mobile number, date of birth, social security number, government ID number, address.)

You should remember and understand that if you share your personal information on any internet platform, it is somehow in risk of being used by a stranger on the internet who might in some worst conditions:

- Be a hacker!

- Pretend to be your friend but wants to take advantage of you!

- Forge his identity to lure you!

- Blackmail you!

- Pretend to be someone you know (like your relative, friend or teacher) and may even exploit you!

So it is essential that you realise why you need to protect your personal information online and be a safe internet citizen. It is indeed not legal for someone else to use your personal or private information for his benefit in a wrong way, and there are cybersecurity departments in every country today that come of great help in punishing those who do so and helping the victims or affected people.

However, it is you who should first know the basics of internet safety and know how to protect himself so that anything like this most possibly doesn't take place at all.

✍ Points to Remember:

- Your personal information includes your name, phone number, address.

- The private information you add on any internet or social media platform is not always safe.

- A stranger who can be a hacker or attacker can misuse the information and later on take advantage of you by causing you a major or minor loss.

- Although there are cybersecurity departments in almost every country, one should take the necessary measures to ensure his/her safety on the internet.

PART TWO

Chapter 4

What is Cyber Security?

In this part, we will take a step ahead in understanding what and how your security online is under risk and what can you do to be safe. Before starting this topic of cybersecurity, let us have a quick look at what the term means that would lead to a better understanding of the concept and the topics ahead:

What is 'Cyber'?

Anything related to the internet, information technology (IT) is 'cyber'. In simpler words, anything that includes or is related to computers, networks, applications or information systems is 'Cyber'.

What is 'Security'?

When someone or something is in the condition of being free from danger or threats, it refers to 'security' and leads to being secure. One takes several different measures to be safe.

Now, what would you call the security that you have to ensure online or on the internet? It is what we call 'Cybersecurity'.

Let's have a look at what all is included in cybersecurity:

- E-safety, internet safety, safety from cyberbullying all come under cybersecurity.

- Securing your information on the internet also comes under cybersecurity.

Merge all the above definitions, and you have a comprehensive description of cybersecurity.

Now let's understand what 'cybersecurity' is by combining the above two definitions:

Cybersecurity refers to all those steps which are taken to be safe and be free from dangers and potential threats on the internet.

Hence, it is essential to know:

- Why one needs to worry about cybersecurity or to be secure in the cyberspace?

- What are the potential threats that can arise on the internet?

- What are some different measures with which one can ensure cybersecurity to protect all the systems that are there in our daily life and are connected to the internet and thus have a probability of harming one's security?

You will find answers to all the questions above in the following topics that will tell you why you need to be safe on the internet, what can go wrong and what can you do to be secure.

✍ **Points to Remember:**

- Cybersecurity includes the measures or steps that are taken to be secure on the internet and avoid threats and dangers.

- Safety from cyberbullying, e-safety, internet safety, and protecting the information of oneself online, all come under cybersecurity.

- In this part of the book, you will understand the basics of cybersecurity and how you can be attacked online.

Chapter 5

What is a Cyber Attack?

It is now essential to know how can your cybersecurity or safety on the internet be harmed, the first thing that might come to your mind would be - *cyber attack*. Let us have a look at what is it and why do hackers perform cyber attacks.

When a person (hacker or attacker) attempts to steal information from a computer or device while also intending to damage or destroy the data stored on it, is what can be termed as a cyber attack.

Who is a Hacker/Attacker?

Someone who breaks into a computer system or device or the network by invading privacy with a purpose to steal, destroy or damage the private and confidential information without having the authority is a hacker/ cyber attacker.

What Could Be the Purpose of a Cyber-Attack?

- Stealing confidential or secret information

- For financial gains (to steal money from your bank account or credit cards)

- Sometimes a hacker might do so to blackmail you and demand money

- To prevent a computer system or website or other services from running

- Sometimes for cyber-bullying

- For a political or religious motive, with an agenda

- Leak your personal information and data.

✍ **Points to Remember:**

- When a person (hacker) to damage or destroy your data, attempts to steal it is called a cyber attack and the one who does it is called an attacker or hacker.

- A cyber attack can also lead to cyberbullying or some other motive to put hindrance in the internet or device activities of someone.

Chapter 6

What is Cyber Bullying?

It might be a widely accepted notion or belief that just because everything today on the internet is readily available and is quite lucrative, it also would be an excellent choice to take the risk of disclosing private or personal information on it with or without knowledge. However, the internet is in no way a safe place without adequate knowledge and understanding of security on it. Unless you are completely aware and well informed about the what(s) and how(s) of the internet, it is better to be on the safer and defensive side than being vulnerable and giving an open door to the people who are looking forward to taking advantage of that.

In simple words to bully, harass, abuse or intimidate someone online is cyber-bullying. If someone is being bullied or harassed or getting abused online, it means he is cyber-bullied.

As you read about cyber attack in the previous chapter, you also must know that cyberbullying is a *type* of cyber attack. You will learn more about other types of cyber attacks in Chapter 9.

The likelihood of you experiencing cyber-bullying online is high as teenagers are the ones who go to the internet often for their assignments, to watch YouTube videos, spend time on social media, play online games. So thus, are an easy target for hackers and attackers. It could involve any of the following:

1. Explicit or non-consensual messages or calls.

2. Constantly sending messages or calling to someone even if they did not ask for it.

3. Having someone's private image & sharing it online (such as social media) without their consent.

4. Posting or sending inappropriate or insulting messages on someone's gender, race or religion.

5. Online threatening.

6. Spreading false rumours about someone.

7. Posting message, pictures, videos to hurt the sentiments of someone.

How Cyber-Bullying May Take Place?

There can be a varied number of ways in which someone can be bullied on the internet (phone, emails, online games, social media). It could be done for blackmailing, insulting or harassing someone, or for any other personal motive. The bully might try to become your friend as a stranger first and try to manipulate you to reveal your private information. Once you fall for the trap, he will start misusing them, and this is how it all starts.

✍ **Points to Remember:**

- Bullying or harassing that takes place on the internet or through internet platforms is what is called cyberbullying and is a type of cyber attack.

- Your personal information on the internet can be used against your safety.

- Strangers on the internet can steal your data and get you in some considerable trouble.

- Kids or teenagers may befriend some stranger and reveal any personal or confidential information and become victims of cyberbullying.

- You may be tricked into a social engineering attack and lose money or reputation or sometimes, both.

- You are always at high risk of losing your important usernames and passwords of different online platforms, and you will see in the coming chapters how the hackers do it.

- It's unfortunate, but it may also result in loss of life sometimes when someone tries to play with your mind and manipulate you into doing something (killer games like 'Blue whale' is just one such example).

Chapter 7

How to Talk to Your Parents if
You're Cyber-Bullied?

I can understand that in case you are going through
cyberbullying or have a friend who has gone through
it, you know very well how difficult it is or can be. Feeling worried and anxious all the time, with a fear residing in you that in case your parents get to know about
it, they will scold you badly and might not come to
help you ever again and instead take away your freedom. Also, you start to solve things as per your mind
thinking it is the right way to do so.

However, it is nothing but fear that makes one think so.
If you have never experienced cyberbullying, that's
great, and I hope this book helps you never fall into
it in future too, but you need to know how can you
encourage yourself or your friends to get out of it if
you or they are suffering from this. It could result in

something severe, so it is essential to speak up and take a stand for yourself to save all that you can before things go completely out of your hands.

Do not feel afraid to tell your parents about it or your relatives you feel close to. Your parents will help you the best they can to get you out of this problem as they can contact the authorities and ask for help in saving you. So it will always be a good lesson for you to remember and learn from. But I know, after unwillingly and unknowingly falling in to the trap of a hacker or attacker who has fooled you into taking out information from you or cheating you, you think it better to not let your parents know, but think of it like this: if something has been broken, it needs to be fixed. Leaving it like that will never help it.

Understanding your feelings that you might go through while being bullied, I want you to consider following tips that will help you communicate better to your parents and ultimately get out from a situation like cyberbullying:

- Go to them when they are free or when you sit with them for dinner and calmly try to tell them that you want to confess and share something. This will give them a slight signal that you are in some trouble and they will most certainly ask you to tell them what happened and understand you.

- Tell them about everything that happened from the start, honestly (about how you came in contact with the person and what all conversation happened between you two and what all he has taken away from you).

- Being honest might be difficult at the beginning, and you might want to twist and turn the facts, but remember it will cause you even more trouble to you later. So while telling your parents, be honest. If you do so, you will feel light and relieved.

- Assure them then no matter what, you are going to share all the proofs with them if something serious has happened.

- Your parents will certainly understand that you have been cheated or bullied. In this generation of technology, even they know that crimes occur on the internet and anyone can become a prey of the hackers.

- If it is possible, ask for a new device or a spare one. Otherwise, you may stop using that device for some time unless proper actions haven't been taken against the criminal.

- Cooperate with them and listen carefully to whatever advice they give you and stick to what you learn from this mistake in future.

✍ Points to Remember:

- It might be difficult for you to take a step and tell your parents if you are cyberbullied and you may want to take things in your hand but, it is the best way if you tell your parents so that they can get the authorities involved if things are worse and save you in time.

- Have courage and always remember that if something has gone wrong, you have to stand for yourself and turn it into right.

- Cyberbullying may happen due to a minor or major mistake that you unknowingly did on the internet or due to your poor sense of judging some stranger too early. Hence, in the next chapter, you will find some necessary and easy steps on how you can handle cyberbullying.

Chapter 8

How to Handle Cyber-Bullying?

So you know that you are being bullied or that your friend has told you he is going through a phase where some stranger or a known person has started to misuse the information against him and is bullying him. It would be best if you were careful of the things to do further immediately and I have provided a list of steps that you should take when you realise you are being bullied:

- Do not respond to any calls/messages from that person who is bullying you.

- Tell your parents immediately.

- Block the person in your mobile call list, from social media account or from gaming account, whichever way he bullied you.

- Do not panic at all and take any step further due to anxiety or fear.

- Immediately change your mobile number or email address or gaming account/profile under the supervision of your parents.

- Immediately change the mobile device with the help of your parents if possible (certainly after the investigation and inquiry by the authorities).

- If cyberbullying has occurred to a friend of you, help him distract by some creative activities (e.g. painting, music, book reading) and also engaging him in some physical activities (e.g. playing their favourite sport, running).

- Reaching out to an expert or a counsellor for further help with your parents' assistance will certainly help you a lot.

- Record all incidents, secure the evidence for further reporting and investigation.

- Lastly, but importantly, do not feel afraid because of the involvement of authorities, nor should you hesitate in telling your parents about the incident due to it. The authorities are there to help you and have advanced methods to find out the person guilty and save you from anything wrong ahead.

- Global media, governments and organisations are continually reaching out to people and children or teenagers of your age to help them realise that if some cyber attack happens to them, they should not be afraid and boldly help the authorities help them and punish the criminal.

Where Can You Report?

Even after taking some measures to protect and keep yourself safe, sometimes for your safety it becomes important to report any such incident to higher authorities to take preventive action and to stop the problem from becoming a disaster.

1. Know and call the government helpline/child protection department, cybersecurity department

which helps in such cases with your parents' guidance.

2. With your parents' supervision, report it to your school teacher or principal of the school.

3. Report the matter to the mobile or internet service provider, relevant law enforcement authorities in your area again with the help of your parents.

✐ **Points to Remember:**

• Never hesitate in telling your parents due to the fear of authorities getting involved, they are there to help you out and punish the guilty.

• Most importantly, take a stand and do not panic at all. Any step that you might take in fear or anxiety might cost you a lot further.

• Record all the incidents and secure the evidence, also do not have any communication with the person bullying you and try to change all the details he has stolen or taken from you by manipulating, all under the supervision of your parents.

Chapter 9

What are the Types of Cyber Attacks?

In the previous chapters, you learned about what is a cyber attack and also read about the most common type of cyber attack- *cyberbullying.*

As mentioned before, cyber attacks are much more than cyberbullying. Let us understand in this chapter some more types of cyber attacks in brief, and what do they mean.

Broadly we can classify the types of cyber-attacks in four types such as:

1. **Malware attacks:**

   o   Viruses

   o   Ransomware

- o   Adware

- o   Spyware

2.   Password attacks

3.   DDoS attack

4.   Social engineering attacks:

- o   Phishing

- o   SMiShing (SMS phishing)

- o   Vishing (Voice phishing)

We will now look at all these terms and understand what they mean so that you can stay well informed and spend a safer cyber time on the internet or your device.

Read each term carefully and do not forget to also aware and inform your friends about them:

1. Malware attacks:

Malware = 'Mal' icious + soft 'ware.'

Software with malicious intent (intending to cause harm and trouble) is Malware. So let's understand its types one by one:

- Viruses:

A virus is a computer program that inserts itself in some other executable computer program code (or in an operating system) stealthily on the user's computer without the user's consent, and when the user executes the program, it causes the virus to spread to other executable files.

A virus requires the computer user to run an already infected program or operating system for the virus to spread, and this is how this malware attack is performed.

- Ransomware:

A 'Ransomware' is another type of 'malware' that prevents the users from accessing their computer systems, either by locking the system's screen or by locking (or encrypting) the users' files unless the user pays a ransom to unlock it. This is a hazardous malware attack.

- Adware:

Knowing about this kind of malware might shock you a bit. This is a very smart malware. The hacker or attacker with this malware tends to trick the user's mind by showing lucrative advertisements on a web browser or while installing something.

These lucrative advertisements are designed in a manner that they already track your online activities, and just when you open a website or download something, these ads will pop up and if you end up clicking on them accidentally or fell into the easy trap of them, considering what is written on the ad is accurate and beneficial to you, then automatically, strange websites will start to pop up, your phone might not respond for a while and unwanted files might get downloaded. This is how this malware is instilled in the user's device, and unfortunately, most of us ignore this.

- Spyware:

This type of malware attack is a significant threat to your online activities. When spyware software installs itself in your device, it starts to track your login credentials on various platforms, bank information and track your internet usage and further sell all these private information to hackers or advertisement agencies. It should be known to you that every year, millions of people lose a lot of money and end up being cyber attacked just because of this malware.

2. Password attacks:

Every time you read an article on cybersecurity or hear from your computer science teacher in the school about it, you must have heard a piece of common advice that everyone talks about: *keeping a strong password and never sharing it with anyone and never to click save password on a website.*

While some of you might be doing so already, most of you will do so now just after what I am going to tell you.

Your password is unsafe. Moreover, it is mostly not in your hands to do anything to make it safe if there is already some spyware or other malware in your device that is keeping track of your online activities or login credentials.

A hacker could easily guess your password with a password dictionary or gain access to your device and the keywords that you type every day and what all do you type while logging in to some website or application and then use it further to steal your information. This is a reason why multi-factor authentication is being used by most businesses and applications (you must be used to the one-time passwords {OTP} that you might find annoying) as they are a safer option towards cybersecurity.

3. DDoS attack:

Before understanding this term, you first need to understand what *DoS* means: DoS or Denial of Service attack is a cyber attack in which the attacker tends to hinder in the access of a real and authorised user into a service or network and stop him from doing so by sending invalid addresses to the server and thus blocking and preventing the trade or service from taking place.

When the same thing is done on a large scale, by flooding the traffic through multiple IP addresses from different sources and distributed networks and devices, it is called as a DDoS attack or *Distributed Denial of Service attack.*

4. Social engineering attacks:

Social engineering is the art of getting the trust of people, obtaining their personal information and manipulating people, so they reveal confidential information.

There are mainly three types of social engineering attacks:

- o Phishing

- o SMiShing (SMS phishing)

- o Vishing (Voice phishing)

• Phishing:

Phishing is a form of cyber-attack where an attacker attempts to obtain sensitive or private information for a malicious purpose, by impersonating himself as someone else. In a phishing attempt, a hacker generally sends emails claiming to be from a bank or police or a reputed company to induce individuals to reveal their personal information (such as your usernames or passwords, credit card and other such details).

- SMiShing (SMS phishing):

  SMiShing is a form of phishing, where the cyber-attackers try to trick you into giving them your private or personal information via a text or SMS message.

  SMiShing is any phishing that involves a text message (e.g. SMS).

- Vishing (Voice phishing):

  A vishing attack is generally carried out just how phishing is done and obviously for the same purpose just that the method used is entirely different including the use of phone calls, voice mail or any voice technology to trick you into revealing and disclosing your personal information.

  Hopefully, now you can understand what the other types of cyber attacks that can happen online and can also realise how important it is to be safe from them so that you do not fall in some problem out of which there is no way to get out. This chapter was to make you aware of what all can go wrong on the internet and what crimes and attacks occur online.

You would certainly not want to be attacked in the cyber world, but the sad truth is really that none of us is safe on the internet. The good thing, however, is that, by taking some simple measures and being careful of a few things, we can lead to a safer and better time on the internet. You will read about these measures and tips in the next chapter.

✍ Points to Remember:

- Generally, cyber attacks can be classified into four types: *malware attacks, password attacks, DDoS (distributed denial of service) attack and social engineering attacks.*

- There are specific malware software that can track your online activities, login credentials and even bank details once they enter in your device through any medium.

- Multi-factor authentication (ex: OTP system) is generally a much safer option, and you should mostly carry out your private details in required circumstances through websites or applications that have this authentication system.

- No matter how unsafe we are on the internet, we can always choose to be safe or protected by following some simple guidelines and by being a little more careful about what we do online.

Passwords:

Use strong passwords wherever a password is required. Follow some basic password rules like:

- *Always* keep your devices password-protected.

- *Create* a *strong* password. E.g. "Mfisoi@8439" (Mfisoi=My family is safe on the internet)

- *Always* use a PIN, Pattern to lock-unlock your mobile/laptop.

- *Change* your passwords at regular intervals.

- *Never* share your passwords with anyone.

For more information on 'password safety' and how to deal with related issues, please refer to Chapter 14.

SMS/Message:

- *Never* send a message to an unknown number.

- *Immediately* delete a message received from a strange number asking for any of your details.

- *Be cautious* and vigilant! If you receive a message/ SMS saying that you've won a lottery and you need to provide your bank account details (generally when a hacker is trying to trick you, it will show some urgency in their messages), ignore or even better, report those numbers.

- *Never* click on a random link you receive in a message/SMS.

Smartphone/Mobile:

- *Always* keep a screen lock (can be PIN/Pattern/ Fingerprint Scanner/Face Unlock).

- *Never* take it lightly if your device is lost. Immediately report it to the authorities.

- *Never* accept a phone call from a strange or unknown number.

- *Never* share your password with anyone.

For more information on mobile safety, please refer to Chapter 11.

E-mail security:

- *Never* open attachments in an email from the people you don't know.

- *Never* click on a link in an email from a stranger/unknown source.

- *Scan* every 'attachment' you download.

- *Tell* your parents/teachers for anything suspicious.

Social media:

- *Keep* your 'friends on social media' limited to your known friends and family members.

- *Be* a responsible internet citizen.

- *Make sure* your parents are also your friends on social media.

- *Do not* publish your personal information on social media.

- *Share* only what you genuinely need to.

For more detailed information on safety on social media, please read Chapter 13.

Websites:

- *Know* the difference between http and https sites (in https, the letter 's' stands for security).

- *Try* to surf https sites only.

- *Although* https sites are safer than http sites, it does not mean that hackers can not trick you. Be vigilant before taking any action on such sites.

- *Most importantly*, stay educated regarding internet and remind yourself about all the dos & don'ts of internet safety.

- *Do not* click on advertisements that seem suspicious and trick you in a quick gain strategy (natural fat loss pills, lottery or prize gifts).

- *Install* Antivirus program in your laptop/mobile.

- *Update* the antivirus software regularly.

- *Backup* your important data regularly.

✍ Points to Remember:

- Although it might seem unlikely but one can ensure internet safety by following some common simple practices. The problem is we think we need to spend a lot of money or when someone tells us what we need to do and we find it to be fundamental, we tend to ignore the advises and instead continue to use the internet as before. But believe me, you will find many news of cybercrime in the newspaper every day and many others that are never mentioned, and it is always better to be safe than sorry, and you can do so by these *'simple'* practices.

- Be careful from strangers, protect your passwords, be responsible for social media and try to surf on safer websites only.

PART THREE

Chapter 11

How to Securely Use Mobile?

In the previous parts and chapters, you learned about the basics of the internet, cyber attacks, cyberbullying and how with some easy steps, you can ensure cybersecurity. In this particular part, you are going to learn about the other dimensions of security that you need to practice whether it is about using electronic devices or other internet platforms.

Let us start by understanding the requirements of the safety of your device and what are the dos and don'ts that you can practise for that:

Mobile Phone Safety:

You must have heard of the game 'BlueWhale' and also of the paedophiles who use Facebook or WhatsApp to lure kids which might have indeed made you feel by now that the internet is quite unsafe. However, I am also sure you must have heard of cases of battery explosion while the phone was on charge. What I mean to say here is that the physical safety of your mobile device is also critical as the safety over the internet.

Physical Safety:

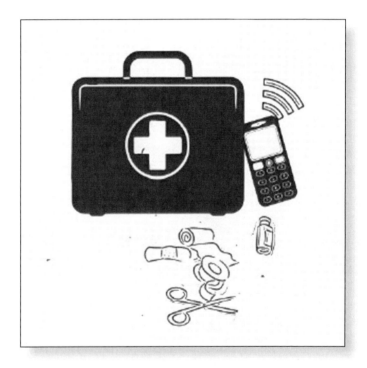

You all must have mobile phones at this age and most certainly take it everywhere you go and use it. Following are some essential dos and don'ts with which you can ensure mobile safety:

Dos:

1. Learn by-heart the emergency dialling numbers of your country/region.

2. Keep your mobile in your pocket or away when you are riding a bike/bicycle or a four-wheeler.

3. Get down on the side of the road if you need to receive a call.

4. Keep your mobile in your pocket before you start to cross the road and be alert to the ongoing traffic.

5. Keep your mobile away from your body when it is charging or while you are sleeping.

6. Use good quality headsets or try to use speaker mode whenever possible.

7. Use good quality, mobile protective cases. Keep Bluetooth, Wi-Fi off when you are not using them.

8. Keep your charger's plug switched off when you are not charging your phone.

9. Be careful of your surroundings while taking a selfie.

Don'ts:

1. Do not share your mobile number with anyone whom you do not know or do not handover your mobile to any stranger.

2. Please do not watch the mobile screen for long hours as it affects not only your eyes but your brain too and also impacts your sleep.

3. Do not use your mobile while you are riding a bike or are on a bicycle.

4. Do not use mobile while crossing a road.

5. Do not use mobile while it is charging.

6. Do not keep your phone on charging when you are sleeping.

7. Please do not keep it under your pillow or near your body while you are sleeping.

8. Do not use your mobile if it has started giving you troubles (get it changed as soon as possible).

9. Please do not use your mobile when it is low on battery or low on signals.

Safety tips for mobile messages:

1. If someone continually sends you vulgar or inappropriate messages, tell your parents, block the sender.

2. Block the sender when you receive any message from a strange or suspicious number (e.g. +0000000, +999999999, +01010101, etc.)

3. But if there are repeated messages, tell your parents, save the messages (you may need the saved copies if your parents plan to report to police) and report if someone sends you vulgar or inappropriate SMS.

4. Make sure the phone is protected with a PIN or a password.

5. Send messages to and receive messages from only people you know and are in your contact list.

6. Only click on a link in a message if the link starts with *https*.

7. Ignore and delete any such forwarded WhatsApp, Facebook and SMS messages that you receive that seem to be trying to spread social chaos by spreading rumours or commenting about someone's identity, colour, race or religion. It can get you in legal troubles.

8. Think before you react to a message in any form (e.g. E-mail, SMS, WhatsApp, Facebook).

9. Keep your school principal's number, your class teacher's number in your mobile.

10. Ignore any call from a strange number which claims to be from your school or the police and is asking about your personal information, e.g. your name, father's name, location, Date of Birth, mobile number, etc.

✍ **Points to Remember:**

- You not only need to be safe on the internet but also practise physical safety measures with your electronic devices.

- Know and learn the emergency numbers of your country/region, always be careful before receiving a call or message from a strange or new phone number and never reveal any private information to any such number without complete knowledge of who it is.

- You might want to take it lightly, but it is a proven fact that electronic devices emit radiations and staying close to them for too long is not good for your health. So keep your phone away when you sleep and never use it when it is charging.

Chapter 12

How to be Safe While Playing Online (Computer or Mobile) Games?

L et's face it; video games are the trend today. After all, who doesn't play them? Be it you or anyone of 30+ age who has to maintain office work, a massive part of our internet population involves itself in video or mobile games to entertain themselves and spend their free time.

Many youngsters have even made good careers in the field of gaming, and this has now become a hobby as well as a field of work and is expected to grow even further over the course of following years. But indeed, it is important to know about what possibly could go wrong on mobile or computer games and what all do you need to know to be safe while playing them.

Personal information:

Your personal information (your full name, mobile number, address) can be misused in one way or another when you are online and connected to a gaming console or merely playing a mobile game online connected to the server, knowingly or unknowingly you may be tricked into providing your personal information which might be used by some hacker later.

Cyberbullying:

Since you do not know who the other person on the other side of the console exactly is, he or she may pretend to be someone else and take advantage of the situation in bullying you in several ways. For example – they may pretend to be living a lavish life with no worries and earning a lot of money, and they can slowly convince you and lure you into doing the things they want, and once you are in their trap, they may bully you or harass you by taking advantage of you. You really might not consider this, but I hope you paid attention while reading Chapter 9 and are very familiar with what can go wrong online and realise the importance of being safe in the cyber world.

Credit Card/Payment Details:

Sometimes when you download a game, even your payment details can be stolen which is stored in your mobile, laptop or gaming console? However, there is another side too where you may lose some money even without having a hacker involved.

Trust me this has happened to me personally. My credit card details were stored in a gaming console for buying some game for my son and on a fine day when I checked my credit card statement, I got to know that there was a charge to download a paid game. When I asked my kid about it, he just denied it and had no idea about it either.

Now the question arises, how to respond to these threats and dangers to your safety? So here is a very simple list for you that will guide you on what to do and what not to do while playing games online:

Dos:

- Always talk to your parents when in doubt or confusion.

- Always download legitimate apps from either the App Store or Play Store only.

- Use a false name while playing a game which does not reflect who you are, how old you or any other information that can reveal your identity.

- Tell your parents if you want to buy any games online and let them decide if it's appropriate for you.

- Know the dangers of being online and how to respond.

- Talk to your parents immediately if anything unusual happens (e.g. someone sending you dirty or vulgar messages).

- Immediately tell your parents and block any such person who sends you any vulgar messages or bullies you while playing a game – fix a time limit for yourself for playing a game on the mobile/ laptop/ XBOX/ PlayStation, etc.

Don'ts:

- Don't accept the friend request from a stranger in an online game.

- Don't (never) share your personal information (your full name, your parent's name, age, date of birth, mobile number, e-mail, address) to other players whom you don't know.

- Don't enter your parent's credit card details into a game without telling them.

- Don't download any game or app yourself.

- Don't play any game where someone/player asks you to do weird things or imagine 'something'.

✍ Points to Remember:

- Video games are the trend today, but it is essential to remember that anything can go wrong on a game as well.

- Your personal information could be harmed or stolen, you could be a victim of cyberbullying, or your bank details might be misused.

- Always play authentic and legitimately safe games that have good reviews and are certified, this will lead to an easier feedback system and communication mechanism with the game developers, in case you sense there is something wrong going on with you.

Chapter 13

How to Be Secure on WhatsApp and Facebook?

There are barely any internet users who regularly use the internet or mobile and do not have apps like WhatsApp or Telegram in their phone to communicate with their friends or relatives. The platforms as mentioned above have a huge user base, and many people all across the world are connected with the help of them.

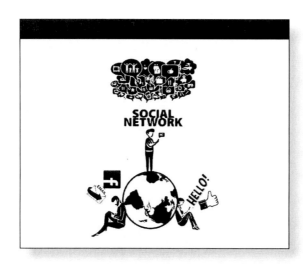

But it is also important to remember always that something might go wrong with these apps and your identity and personal information might be hampered or be at risk. It is your responsibility to know what all that could be and how can you avoid them and use these apps safely.

WhatsApp:

What Can Go Wrong?

A message received on WhatsApp from an unknown person or a strange number can bring in numerous dangers if taken for granted and not dealt appropriately.

Suppose you get a message with a link which asks you to provide your bank details or your personal information or it shows that you have won a lottery or an Amazon gift voucher.

Have you ever thought what could go wrong if you clicked on that link? The hacker on the other side can install an app on your mobile device without you even knowing about it and have all the control of your mobile.

You might be asked to click the link to download an 'amazing app' or a 'free mobile game', and you install that app on your mobile to get something for '*free*'.

You also might have heard about some addictive games which incite children into doing unethical things and promote harmful activities. The people behind such apps generally use the above method to reach out to potential victims via a link in a message as you can not download these from Play Store or App Store. Hence it is vital to be aware and to keep children aware of what can go wrong and how to avoid this from happening and how to protect yourself as well.

Here are Some Dos and Don'ts:

Dos:

- Only read messages received from your known contacts or people already in your contact list.

- Let your parents know for any such messages (which are received from unknown people). Request them to block it and learn yourself to block it too.

- Anytime you doubt any message/call, ask your parents and always keep your mobile password/PIN protected.

- Only click the links received from your known contacts and which start with 'https'.

- Be attentive and block the sender of the message which you received just now and you feel it has a sense of urgency (e.g. a message saying "please immediately provide your name and account number to avoid any charges").

Children (Don'ts):

- Do not click on any link in a message received by an unknown contact.

- Do not share your passwords with anyone except your parents.

- Do not receive a WhatsApp call from an unknown number (or number not in your contact list).

- Do not click or open those links which start with 'http'.

- Do not share your personal information with any stranger. Your name, father's name, DOB, E-mail, mobile number, address are all your 'Personal Information'. You should not share this information with any stranger on WhatsApp who claims to be from your school, government offices or your distant relative, etc.

- Do not forward those messages to anyone in person or a WhatsApp group, commenting on someone's identity, race, religion, colour or country.

Facebook:

We all are living in the 'information age', the 'Internet era', the 'Cyber World' that is connected by various social media websites and apps; Facebook is one of them. While Facebook has helped a lot being in touch with our near and dear ones, sharing our thoughts with them and communicating, helped businesses flourish. But at the same time, it has brought another set of dangers especially for kids and teenagers- cyberbullying, and dangerous game requests to name few.

Let's try to understand with easy steps as to how can you make sure that you are safe online especially while on Facebook? What are the dangers and what are the things that you should avoid for always staying secure?

What Can Go Wrong on Facebook?

- A stranger can send you a friend request, once accepted he could track where you are, what you're up to, when are you alone and take advantage of it.

- Your teachers or parents may read your comments; they may see what you're sharing or liking online.

- Nowadays hiring companies are also checking your social media presence and other details before you are hired for a job. So be very careful of what you're commenting, liking and sharing as you don't know when you may lose your career even before you've started one.

- It might lead to cyberbullying if you shared any of your secret with a stranger.

- A stranger befriended on Facebook can share your details with kidnappers.

- A negative or wrong comment can offend someone.

- If your teachers or parents read your comments which are not good or they may also see what you've shared or liked online and if any of these are not good or offensive, they may not feel good about it and ask you to check your behaviour.

- Someone can even use photos of someone else to create a fake profile on some site so that they can misuse it as they want.

How to Respond?

Dos:

- Be polite and respectful to others.

- Do comment and share what inspires others, spread positivity.

- Ask your parents or some elder relative you feel friendly towards if confused about anything.

- Inform your parents if someone bullies you or sends vulgar or irrelevant messages – block the person from your account immediately.

- Immediately delete the comment on your photo or post which you think is not reasonable or not appropriate.

- Always keep your mobile password/PIN protected and do not share your passwords with anyone except your parents.

- Share all above Dos and Don'ts points with your parents and friends and educate others.

- Read articles, watch videos on online security so that you're aware of new attack types and how to deal with them.

Don'ts:

- Don't accept the friend request from a stranger (you should not befriend anyone you don't know personally).

- Don't post your personal information (your mobile number, address, etc.) online.

- Don't post your whereabouts (e.g. Hurrah mom-dad away for two days, it's just my Xbox and me now alone at home-feeling excited).

- Don't post or comment something online if you think this is going to hurt someone's feelings.

If you think all these tips or dos and don'ts are too basic and clichéd, you most certainly to an extent are correct but in no way, these tips can be or should be ignored. Pick out newspapers or search online about the news of cyber-crime, you will easily be able to see that most of the crimes, if not all have happened online because the victim or the person affected, did not follow some of the tips above.

It is important to realise that you don't need to do a lot for your safety, just doing a little in the right manner, will keep you secure.

✍ **Points to Remember:**

- Social networks and communication apps are very widely used today. Some of the most famous ones are Facebook and WhatsApp and to be safe on them, is again your responsibility. Be aware and careful of opening or clicking on links that have been sent to you via some stranger.

- You must have heard of the recent Facebook data leak matter. It is true that even on these huge businesses or social networks with heavy securities for the users, sometimes few things might go wrong. Hence, it is always better to not put any information online that if lost can be misused against you or might cause you harm.

Chapter 14

How to Create and Protect
Your Passwords?

Passwords are one of the most essential part of any-thing that exists on the internet. They help in pro-tecting your identity, files and media, etc. But in today's time when cracking passwords and tracing the login details of devices is a common practice by certain hack-ers or attackers, it is essential to know the basics of creating and protecting your passwords. Here are some dos and don'ts of creating passwords:

Dos:

1. Use a strong password.

2. If your device has biometric security (Fingerprint scanner/ Face unlock/Iris Scanner), then use them.

3. Change your passwords every three months at least.

4. Keep your passwords to yourself.

5. Choose a password that cannot be easily guessed or hacked.

6. Use different passwords for different accounts (similar but a bit distinct, so that you can remember them).

7. Make a password that is long and complex but is easy to remember
(e.g. MyCityIsBest&Biggest_4535) – It's even better to use nonsensical words or phrases
(e.g. Crooked&Booked4Crime_199).

8. Update all your apps/software regularly.

9. Change the default passwords generated by apps or websites immediately.

10. Use a combination of Uppercase, Lowercase, Numbers, Special Characters, Spaces (if allowed).

Don'ts:

1. Do not keep your device without passwords.

2. Do not use a weak password if you are using one.

3. Do not share your passwords with anyone.

4. Do not use the same passwords for all the accounts.

5. Do not fall for Phishing, Vishing or SMiShing and disclose your password.

6. Please do not write your passwords down any-where (try to remember them only).

7. Do not use your personal information (e.g. Your name, address, email, date of birth, etc) in your passwords.

8. Do not use your passwords on devices which are not yours or which you do not trust.

9. Do not use your passwords on networks (e.g. Wi Fi, Hot Spot) which are not yours or which you do not know.

10. Do not use default passwords generated by apps or websites.

✍ Points to Remember:

- Passwords protect any data online and create a barrier on someone from accessing them, but it is still important to learn how to create a password and even keep it safe as well.

- Never have the same password for all your data or on platforms, you may keep it similar but never the same.

- Try to make your passwords difficult and random to make them tough to guess and so that even if someone tries to access to some of your data and guess the password, you can get notified and quickly take action.

Chapter 15

Dos & Don'ts of Internet

Internet Safety:

Most of the times when you are using a mobile, you are connected to a network (e.g. your service provider) or the internet. As mobile technology and the internet has evolved, the threats of being on the internet have also grown significantly. Every other day we read or listen to many such incidents, hence in below mentioned few

steps, I'll be talking about the safety tips for using mobile and internet, to sum up, all that I need to bring your attention to in this chapter:

Dos:

1. Be vigilant; be careful.

2. Talk less and use texting for short conversations.

3. Make sure the phone is protected with a PIN or a password.

4. Reject any call from a strange or suspicious number (e.g. +0000000, +999999999, +01010101, etc.).

5. Tell your parents and report if you think you are being bullied or someone calls you with different numbers every time and bothers you.

6. Keep the Bluetooth and Wi-Fi off when not in use.

7. Call only when signal strength is good. If not, wait if it's not urgent.

8. Also, be safe while playing online games or while using WhatsApp or be safe while using Facebook.

9. Download only from official websites, App Store or Play Store.

Don'ts:

1. Do not talk for long hours; use texting instead whenever and wherever possible.

2. Do not leave your mobile unattended and away from your sight.

3. Do not talk on the mobile while it is charging.

4. Do not talk to strangers.

5. Do not hide from your parents or teachers if someone calls you repeatedly and bothers you.

6. Do not receive or dial a phone call when it is low on battery or the signals are low.

7. Do not keep your Wi-Fi or Bluetooth on all the time.

8. Do not respond to a call which claims to be from your school, college or police and is asking about your personal information, e.g. your name, father's name, location, Date of Birth, mobile number, etc.

9. Do not ignore cyber bullies, learn to take a stand against them and teach them a lesson.

✍ Points to Remember:

- The threats and dangers of being on the internet are increasing rapidly over the years; hence you should be vigilant and careful about everything that you do online. Please always remember, just because the internet is easy to use and surf on, doesn't mean it is also safe.

- While using any application or software, be careful of what you read or what pops up. The hackers or attackers are ingenious and can trick you in a way you never thought.

- Please share with your relatives and friends as well whatever you have learned about cyber security and also guide them to be a safe internet citizen.

Made in United States
North Haven, CT
10 February 2023